WELCOME TO FORT GEORGE

Fort George is one of the most outstanding fortifications in Europe. It was built in the wake of the 1745–6 Jacobite Rising as part of a concerted effort by George II's government to ensure that the Highland clans would never again rise in support of the exiled Stuart dynasty. Planned as an impregnable army base, the fort was designed and built to the highest standards of artillery fortification. Within its sophisticated defences were buildings providing all that was necessary for its garrison of almost 2,000 men.

Yet by the time Fort George was completed in 1769, the Highlands were peaceful. The fort continued in use, however, as a training base for regiments recruited in Scotland, especially the Highlands. From 1881 until 1964 it was the home depot of the Seaforth Highlanders (amalgamated with the Cameron Highlanders in 1961). Today, the fort continues to serve the needs of the modern British Army.

Above: Lieutenant-General William Skinner (1700–80), the engineer and designer of Fort George.

CONTENTS

Left: This aerial view shows the precision engineering and symmetry of Fort George, with its 1km-long rampart (main defensive wall) and bastions (projecting fortifications).

FORT GEORGE AT A GLANCE

Fort George is the most tangible reminder left to us of the turbulent times of the Jacobite wars of the early 18th century. Following the overthrow in 1689 of James VII of Scotland and II of England, the Jacobites (from *Jacobus*, Latin for James) rose in rebellion five times in their attempt to return the Stuarts to the throne of Great Britain and Ireland. Their fifth and final rising ended in humiliating defeat at Culloden on 16 April 1746, within 5 miles (8km) of where Fort George would soon be built.

Fort George, named after George II (1727–60), is one of the outstanding artillery fortifications anywhere in Europe. Its elaborate and formidable bastioned defences survive complete, as do all the original garrison buildings. Today, guns still bristle from its ramparts, and soldiers still drill in the barrack square.

Right: Fort George jutting out into the Moray Firth, with Fortrose on the far side and snow-covered Ben Wyvis in the distance.

THE ARCHITECTURE OF WAR

10 IMPREGNABLE SHIELD
The main rampart, over 1km round, encloses an area the size of five football pitches.

10 MIGHTY BASTIONS
Projecting from the rampart, the bastions supported heavy guns that could cover every blind spot.

6 ELABORATE OUTWORKS
Designed to protect the fort from landward attack, they are among the best examples of military architecture in Europe.

10 SENTRY BOXES
Provided patrols with shelter on stormy nights.

GUNS AND WEAPONS

11 AWESOME FIREPOWER
The original armament comprised over 80 heavy guns. The guns here today are reminders of the fort's defensive might.

Whole Powder Barrel to hold 100lbs

16 GRAND MAGAZINE
The magazine housed 2,500 barrels of gunpowder.

18 THE SEAFIELD COLLECTION
A priceless collection of 18th-century military equipment.

REGIMENTAL ASSOCIATIONS

A SOLDIER'S LIFE

A GUIDED TOUR

This tour guides you around mighty Fort George, a vast complex of artillery fortifications and garrison buildings. The fortifications are largely accessible to visitors, but because Fort George still serves as an Army base, most of the garrison buildings are not open to the public. They can all, however, be viewed from the outside.

The tour takes you firstly around the fort's formidable defences – among the best preserved in Europe – before passing on to the garrison buildings. It begins at the outworks beyond the east (landward) front. If you have already passed through these as far as the visitor centre on the ravelin, you may wish to return to this section as you leave the fort at the end of your visit.

You can also view the outworks from vantage points on the ravelin and the Prince of Wales's bastion. To begin your tour at the ravelin, turn to page 6.

Map key

1 Ravelin guardhouse
2 Ravelin
3 Principal bridge
4 Guardrooms
5 Parade
6 'Black Hole', or prison
7 Prince of Wales's bastion
8 Duke of Cumberland's bastion
9 Governor's house
10 Regimental museum
11 Point battery
12 Garrison chapel
13 Barrack square

14 Provision stores
15 Historic barrack rooms
16 Grand magazine
17 The Seafield Collection of Arms
18 First World War memorial
19 South casemated curtain and sallyport
20 Prince William Henry's bastion
21 Harbour
22 Prince Frederick William's demi-bastion
23 Duke of Marlborough's demi-bastion

24 Prince Henry Frederick's bastion
25 North casemated curtain and sallyport
26 Dog cemetery
27 Casemates
28 Artillery block
29 Staff block
30 Workshops
31 Ordnance stores
32 Seaforth's regimental institute
33 Principal ditch
34 Glacis

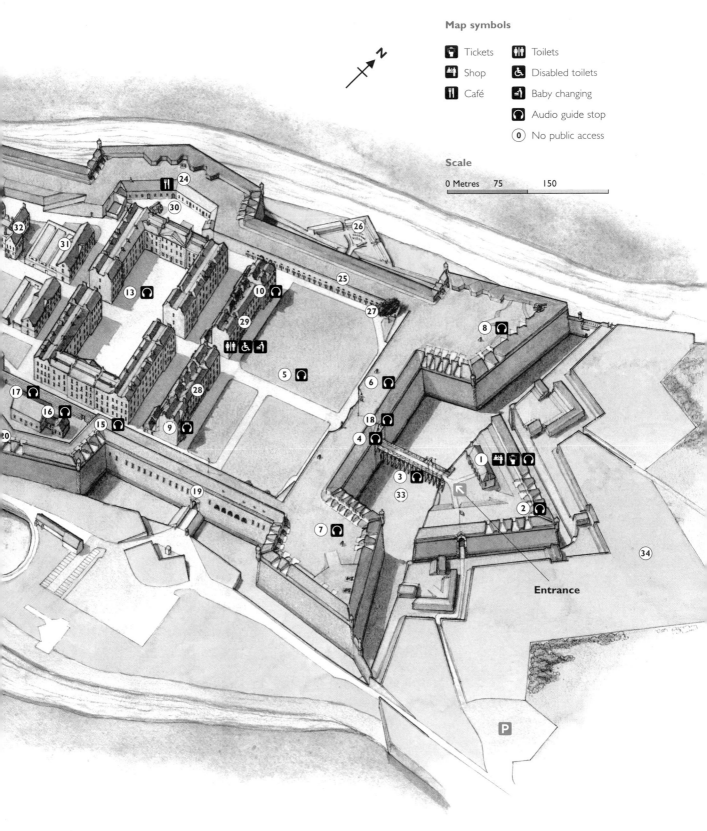

Map symbols

🎫	Tickets	🚻	Toilets
🛍	Shop	♿	Disabled toilets
🍴	Café	🚼	Baby changing
		🎧	Audio guide stop
		⓪	No public access

Scale

0 Metres   75   150

Entrance

THE OUTWORKS AND RAVELIN

Fort George is built on a shingle peninsular jutting into the Moray Firth. The sea protects the fort on three sides, leaving its eastern, landward, approach as the most vulnerable. This explains the far more elaborate defences on the eastern side, the first to be built at the fort, between 1748 and 1753.

The outworks consist of a number of obstacles built to prevent the enemy from bringing heavy guns close enough to bear on the rampart, or main defensive wall. They also enabled the garrison to move about on foot beyond the main rampart in relative safety, as well as providing protected areas for them to gather to counter-attack.

The first obstacle the enemy would encounter was the glacis, a gently sloping grassy bank 50m wide, zigzagging across the neck of the promontory. Constructed of earth excavated from the great ditches behind it, the glacis was intended to soak up incoming artillery shot. The roads to Nairn and Inverness passed through the glacis; the latter now forms the main visitor path into the fort.

Behind the glacis was the covered way, a defensive line that was protected from enemy fire by the brick parapet wall at the rear of the glacis. The defenders would use the earthwork bank as a step from which to fire their muskets or trench mortars. Immediately in front of them was a timber palisade, or fence, of sharpened fir trees, 2.5m high. The palisade was made in sections so that soldiers could push a stretch over when they needed to scale the parapet.

Prince Edward's Ravelin (named after George II's second grandson) was the strongest of the outworks. Its triangular shape was dictated by the need to give flanking cover along its outer ditch for the guns on the fort's frontal bastions (fortified projections from the main wall). The ravelin guardhouse was built in 1753 to guard the main approach into the fort. It now houses the visitor centre.

Opposite: The imposing point of Prince Edward's Ravelin. The ravelin has a rampart facing landwards with embrasures, or openings, for eight guns, a sentry box and firing-steps. The rear has no such feature – the reasoning being that the ravelin would be of no offensive use to an enemy should they capture it.

Below left: The ravelin guardhouse. The guards were based in the central section, and their officers in the pavilions at either end. The arcading enabled officers to inspect the guard under cover.

Below: Part of the reconstructed palisade, or fence of sharpened timber stakes, behind the firing wall.

I SHALL BE EXTREMELY GLAD
THEY WOULD DO IT, BECAUSE
I LOOK UPON THAT FORT
TO BE IMPREGNABLE.

Lord Ligonier, commander-in-chief of the
British Army, on hearing in 1759 that
the French were contemplating
attacking Fort George

THE PRINCIPAL GATE

The principal gate was completed by 1756, but the great studded doors were not hung until ten years later. The gate was intended to impress those passing through it, its contrasting yellow and red sandstone Doric pilasters supporting a pediment emblazoned with the royal arms of George II.

The huge ditch in front of the gate was excavated between 1748 and 1753, the soil being used to create the high mounds forming the ravelin and bastions. Measuring 300m long and 50m wide in its central section, the ditch was capable of being flooded at high tide, the water pouring through sluices in the end walls, called batardeaux. The ditch would normally have been kept dry, however, a wet ditch being a mixed blessing in time of siege since it could inhibit the movement of defenders around the outworks and impede counter-attack.

The bridge over the ditch, constructed in 1766, originally had two drawbridges along it. The one near the ravelin is a 1980 reconstruction based on Lieutenant-General William Skinner's original drawing. The other was immediately in front of the principal gate.

THE GUARDROOMS AND PARADE

The cobbled passage behind the gate led to an arcaded vestibule with guardrooms. The smaller of the two, on the right as you enter, was for the officers of the guard, and the larger, on the left, for the guard itself. The room beyond the officers' guardroom was the prison, known in the 18th century as the 'black hole'. This became redundant in Victorian times when new cells were formed in the provision stores.

Immediately inside the fort lies the parade, a broad sweep of grass that was used for events such as ceremonial parades. It was otherwise reserved for the staff officers, their wives and families residing in the impressive buildings at the far side.

You now have a choice – you can either turn left or right and walk up the ramps to view the ramparts (see page 10), or you can continue straight ahead and visit the garrison buildings inside the fort (turn to page 12).

Above (top): George II's coat of arms, set over the principal gate, contain, from the top left quarter going clockwise: Scotland impaling England, France, the House of Hanover and Ireland. The royal arms of Scotland are inaccurate: they should contain a double border (tressure) around the insignia.

Above: Arches outside the guardrooms on either side of the principal gate.

Opposite: The bridge and principal gate from the Ravelin.

THE RAMPART AND BASTIONS

The fort's main defence was the formidable rampart, which was equipped with over 70 guns. About a kilometre long, it consisted of bastions and demi-bastions formed of earth cast up from the surrounding ditch and encased in sloping stone walls, designed to absorb artillery shot.

All the bastions had four sides, two facing outwards and two covering the flanks of main wall, to give the gun-crews complete cover of the rampart and approach. The two largest bastions were those named after the Prince of Wales (the future George III) and the Duke of Cumberland (the victor at Culloden). Both bastions flanked the principal gate and faced over the outworks to the landward side, where the main threat was anticipated in the 1750s. Circular stone boxes at the bastions' corners enabled sentries to keep watch in comparative safety.

Under the rampart running west from these two main bastions were bomb-proof storage cellars called casemates. Beyond were sallyports, or side gates, to be used during sieges for counter-attack; defensive places of arms were located immediately outside each sallyport for this purpose. The place of arms beyond the north sallyport was later turned into a dog cemetery for regimental mascots and officers' pets.

Above: The sentry boxes on top of the Prince William Henry's bastion. Most of the bastions were named after close relatives of George II.

Below: The Prince of Wales's bastion, as seen from the outworks. This view demonstrates the complex interplay of ramparts, bastions and other structures built to shield the fort.

Midway along the long stretches of rampart were two more bastions. Prince William Henry's bastion (after George II's third grandson), along the south rampart, had openings for nine guns. Prince Henry Frederick's bastion (after George II's fourth grandson), along the north rampart, enclosed the workshops for carpenters, blacksmiths and wheelwrights around a courtyard.

The far west end of the fort comprised the point battery, flanked by Prince Frederick William's demi-bastion (after George II's youngest grandson) and the Duke of Marlborough's demi-bastion (the only bastion not named after a member of the royal family). Within the point battery were four gun ports for 32-pounders – among the very few changes made to the original designs of the fort, which probably reflected growing concern about a French attack from the sea.

Above left: A traversing gun on the Point battery.

Above top: The north sallyport, which today leads to the dog cemetery, a gravestone from which is shown underneath.

DOLPHINS AT FORT GEORGE

The Point battery is now the best place from which to view bottlenose dolphins, as well as harbour porpoises and minke whales, playing and feeding in the Moray Firth. Bottlenoses are the most numerous cetaceans in the Firth. The most likely time to see them is on a calm day between April and September, about one hour before and after high and low tide. Harbour porpoises are smaller than dolphins and have a smaller, triangular fin. Minke whales, on the other hand, are much bigger, growing to around 10m in length. They tend to be seen at the end of the summer.

THE GARRISON BUILDINGS

The garrison buildings, which took 14 years to build (from 1753 to 1767), were designed to accommodate almost 2,000 soldiers. Lieutenant-General Skinner planned the buildings symmetrically and generously surrounded them with open space. The panoramic view on entering the fort today is little different from the one visitors saw in 1769 – the most noticeable difference is the modern tarmac road.

Above: The west end of the parade ground, flanked by the artillery and staff blocks. All the buildings inside the fort were laid out to a symmetrical plan.

(1) The governor's house, now the officer's mess; **(2)** a 19th-century view of the artillery and staff blocks; and **(3)** a rainwater hopper on one of the barrack blocks beyond, with the royal cipher of King George III and the date 1761.

THE ARTILLERY AND STAFF BLOCKS

The blocks, which grace the far (west) side of the parade, are fine examples of Georgian architecture. They provided accommodation for the gunners manning the fort's artillery and the staff officers – such as the ordnance storekeeper, ordnance paymaster and surgeon – who were permanently based at the fort. The pavilions projecting from either end provided houses for the governor and lieutenant-governor and fort major, their pediments and porches emphasising the higher status of their occupants.

The governor's house is now the officers' mess, whilst the lieutenant-governor and fort major's house serves as the home of the regimental museum of the Highlanders (formerly the Queen's Own Highlanders, an amalgamation of the Seaforth & Cameron Highlanders). Fort George was the depot of the Seaforths from 1880 until 1964, and is their spiritual home. The museum is a permanent memorial to the thousands of soldiers who served in the various Highland regiments since the late 18th century. It contains over 11,000 objects, and is free to enter for visitors to the fort.

Below: Children play in the foreground of this photograph, taken on the parade ground on 17 August 1903 at a presentation of medals to members of the 1st Battalion of the Cameron Highlanders who had fought in the South African, or Boer, war.

THE BARRACKS

The two barrack piles were intended to house two field battalions – 1,600 men in all. The projecting central and terminal pavilions in each pile were for officers and the remainder for the non-commissioned officers (NCOs) and rank-and-file. (If you stand in the barrack square, you can easily distinguish officers' accommodation from that of the men by looking at the window panes – the officers' window panes were larger, to let in more light.) Regular drill was carried out in the barrack square between the two ranges.

LIFE IN THE BARRACKS

Much of the barracks is still occupied by soldiers. However, three barrack rooms in the south pile have been recreated to show what living conditions might have been like for officers and soldiers stationed here at different times. (These recreated barrack rooms are accessible from the south side, not from the barrack square.) The first of these rooms shows a soldiers' barrack quarters in 1780. Eight privates from the 42nd Royal Highlanders cooked, ate and slept in the one room, two to a bed. There was no communal mess in those days, and toilet facilities were basic. The men drew their daily rations from the provision stores and cooked for themselves. One in a hundred men was allowed to be married 'on the strength', with his wife, children and pets living-in; the wife received half rations in return for doing domestic chores. The only concession to privacy was a blanket drawn across their corner of the barrack room.

The second room is a soldiers' barrack room of 1868. Five privates occupied the room, each sleeping in a single bed. They no longer had to cook or toilet in their room, for communal messing and latrine facilities were now routine. Married quarters too had become the norm 'in order that the men be not disturbed by the noyse of the children'. The third room, an officer's room set in 1813, at the height of the Napoleonic Wars, is noticeably lighter and more airy than the other two, but is far from luxurious. The life of a serving officer was as uncertain as that of his men, his pay barely sufficient to keep him in the manner expected of him by his regiment. All that he possessed, including his furniture, had to be capable of being transported from one base to another as well as on campaign.

Above: A date stone showing the completion of the southern barrack pile in 1763.

Opposite: Clockwise, from top: the barrack square in 1895; a detail from the officer's room of 1813; a fold-up bed and bayonet from the 1868 barrack room; the 1780 barrack room; and the west elevation of the north barracks.

Above: A canvas knapsack belonging to a soldier from the 97th Inverness-shire Regiment, part of the Seafield Collection (see page 18).

ENTRANCE TO SHIFTING ROOM

2672 BARRELS

Above: The grand magazine, stacked high with replica powder barrels. **(1)** An air vent fitted with a copper-sheathed timber shutter; **(2)** the doorway into the magazine; and **(3)** an indication of the magazine's capacity – over 2,500 barrels of gunpowder.

THE GRAND MAGAZINE

The risk attached to storing gunpowder had been graphically demonstrated during the Jacobite Rising in 1745–6, when the powder magazine at Fort Augustus, built at the southern end of Loch Ness, suffered a direct hit during a siege and exploded. Skinner learnt from that experience – every detail of Fort George's grand magazine was designed to minimise such an event happening again. The magazine was tucked into one of the bastions and divided from the rest of the fort by a tall blast wall. This reduced the possibility of fire entering the magazine enclosure accidentally, and helped contain a blast should the magazine explode.

ROBUST DESIGN

The grand magazine had to be strong enough to withstand a direct hit from a 13-inch mortar bomb, the most powerful armament then available. It also had to keep the powder cool and dry. Hence the massive brick vaults supporting the slated roof and the wall vents beneath the raised timber floor. In order to eliminate sparks, no iron was used in its construction. All the doors, vent shutters and rainwater goods were either made from, or sheathed in, copper, and the flooring and barrel racks were fixed by wooden dowels. Even the men working in the magazine had to change into special shoes and clothes containing no iron fittings or buttons before entering. The final precaution was the provision of large water tanks (now gone) on the outside wall of the magazine, close to the door leading into the central corridor separating the magazine itself from the cooperage, where barrels were made and repaired.

Take any person prisoner entering the magazine if they do not open the door on the first turn of the key. To prevent people from smoking or carrying fire near his post and hinder idle people from lounging near.

Instruction given to the sentry on guard at the magazine door

Above: An exact replica gunpowder barrel in the magazine.

Left: The grand magazine was built to withstand a direct hit from a mortar bomb.

THE SEAFIELD COLLECTION

The Seafield Collection is a priceless assortment of late 18th-century arms and military equipment, on display in the grand magazine.

During the French Revolutionary Wars (1793–1803), with the threat of invasion ever-present, Sir James Grant of Grant, Lord Lieutenant of Inverness-shire, raised and equipped several regiments locally to help the war effort. They included the Strathspey Fencible Regiment, the 97th Regiment of Foot, the Inverness-shire Volunteers and the Inverness-shire Militia.

The Seafield Collection includes a drum and grenadier cap of the Strathspey Fencibles, India-pattern muskets with bayonets (the standard infantry weapon from 1794), pikes issued to the Strathspey Company of the Inverness-shire Volunteers as an economy measure at a time when muskets were in short supply, ammunition pouches (of 'stoutest blackened calf skin … to turn the severest rain'), knapsacks (of 'stout canvas, painted') issued to the men of the 97th, brass shoe-buckles and an assortment of officers' swords. When Sir James tried to sell the collection in 1810, after the invasion threat was over, he found ready takers for the clothing – all except the grenadier caps, that is – but thankfully none for the rest. The collection came into state care in 1978 from the estate of the Dowager Countess of Seafield, Sir James's descendant.

Above: A rope-tensioned side drum, made by Robert Home of London in about 1790 for the Strathspey Fencibles.

Below: A detail from an India-pattern flintlock musket.

1

2   **3**   **4**

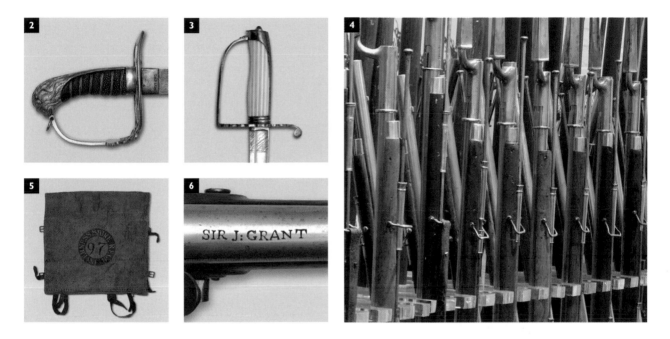

5   **6**

7

1 Non-commissioned officer's brass-hilted broadsword

2 Lion-headed brass hilt from an officer's spadroon sword

3 Brass and ivory hilt from an officer's spadroon sword

4 A detail from the stand of Napoleonic Wars-era muskets and pikes that forms a major part of the Seafield Collection

5 Knapsack of the 97th Regiment of Foot

6 Detail showing the stamp of Sir James, the commanding officer, on a musket barrel

7 Grenadier's bearskin cap, issued to Grenadier Donald Smith

THE ORDNANCE AND PROVISION STORES

The twin ordnance stores were built between 1759 and 1761. These huge warehouses stored shot and shell on their ground floors and an armoury above. Behind them were open courtyards. In 1782, with the garrison reduced to one battalion and a company of Invalids (see page 37), the north store was converted into a military hospital, with the mortuary located in the yard behind.

Beyond the ordnance stores was another open space, used for parade practice. The north side was built on in 1934, when the Regimental Institute was added for use by the Seaforth Highlanders – the only entirely new structure erected within the fort since 1769. In the rampart walls on either side of the parade were the latrines – two for officers and two for NCOs and men.

Above: The provision stores, with the fort's chapel visible through the archway. The south store, to the left of the arch, was gutted by fire in 1952; since that time it has served as the sergeants' mess.

The provision of latrines was clearly a long running problem. In an order issued in 1797 it was reported that: 'As the drains and necessaries are now cleaned and a new necessary erected at the harbour, there can be no apology for the dirty situation at the ramparts.' These 'necessary houses' became redundant during the 19th century when ablution-blocks were added to the barracks.

The two provision stores, built between 1760 and 1762, were the domain of the baker (to the left of the archway) and the brewer (to the right). Both had residences in the end pavilions, above their bakery and brewery. The ranges in between were used to store grain and other food provisions, given out to the soldiers as rations. Coal was stored in the yards to the rear, alongside the baker's and brewer's cart-sheds and stables. The north store was converted into prison cells in the 19th century, replacing the outdated 'black hole' beside the principal gate. The archway linking the two stores was evidently intended to support an eye-catching clock tower, but whether it was ever built is not clear.

Below: The original 1762 plan for the provision stores. The stores provided enough food and drink for the 2,000-strong garrison.

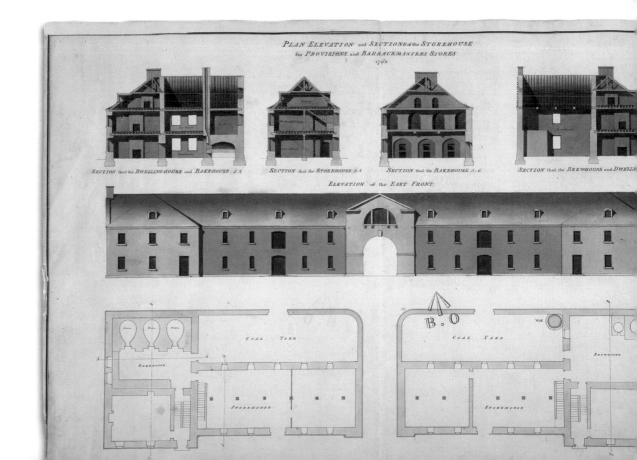

THE CHAPEL

This 'pritty' chapel was the one significant departure from Lieutenant-General Skinner's original scheme for the fort, work on it beginning only in 1763. The original intention had been for the garrison to attend the local kirk at Kirkton of Ardersier, close beside the road to Nairn. The minister of Kirkton served as the fort chaplain until 1777, when the duty passed to the minister of Ardersier. The cemetery at Kirkton, however, continued in use as the garrison cemetery, and many fine tombstones can still be seen there.

Above: The interior of the chapel, which continues to serve the spiritual needs of the regiments stationed at Fort George today.

The handsome building is thought to have been designed by one of the Adam brothers, perhaps Robert himself (see page 32). The exterior has a polygonal chancel at the east end and a squat, battlemented west tower. The central nave has flanking rounded stair towers. The interior has a gallery around three sides. The rank-and-file soldiers occupied the nave, whilst their officers and families had box-pews in the west gallery. Visitors were permitted to sit in the side galleries. Vestries once occupied the east bays of the nave aisles, entered from doors in the east end walls; these have now been replaced by memorial windows.

The unusual three-decker pulpit on the left side of the chancel originally stood in the middle, but was first moved to the right side in the 1930s, when the church doubled as the garrison school. Now missing its sounding board at the top, it housed the minister (top), the reader (centre) and the precentor (bottom), who led the singing. The Latin inscription over the chancel arch reads: 'George III, by the grace of God King of Great Britain, France and Ireland, 1767.'

Above: A medallion portraying Robert Adam (1728–92), the possible designer of the chapel, on display in the Scottish National Portrait Gallery, Edinburgh.

Below: Clockwise from top right: regimental badge of the Seaforth Highlanders at the west end of the chapel; stained glass detail; the three-decker pulpit; and the chapel from the west.

THE STORY OF
FORT GEORGE

When it is finished, one may venture to say that it will be the most considerable fortress and the best situated in Britain.

Lieutenant-Colonel James Wolfe,
veteran of Culloden and future hero of Quebec, 1751

On 16 April 1746, on wet and windswept Drummossie Moor, a little to the east of Culloden House, Prince Charles Edward Stuart's soldiers were mercilessly cut down by the army of George II, commanded by his younger brother, William, duke of Cumberland. While the battle of Culloden proved the last gasp for Jacobitism, it determined the Crown to ensure that such a rising would never again find support among the Highland clans.

The measures taken included the construction of mighty Fort George, which began two years after Culloden. The garrison fortress took 21 years to build and cost more than twice the estimated budget – many millions of pounds at today's prices. By the time it was completed, Jacobite support for the exiled Stuart dynasty had evaporated, and the fort's guns never had to fire a single shot in anger. However, the money was not wasted for a new role was soon found for the fort – as a recruiting base and training ground for the new Highland regiments needed to fight across the burgeoning British empire. Today, Fort George still serves as an active Army base.

Left: A late 18th-century depiction of Fort George, as seen from a stormy Moray Firth.

THE JACOBITE THREAT

Disruption in the Highlands was nothing new – the different culture, derived in part from the harsh environment, had caused concern to the central government of Scotland since the middle ages. What were seen as unruly customs and a lack of respect for authority, coupled with an ancient way of life, bred suspicion in the minds of the Highlanders' southern neighbours.

It was in the 1650s, however, that serious disaffection broke out among the Highland clans over the foreign military occupation ordered by Oliver Cromwell. To impose order, Cromwell introduced a police state, and set about building formidable fortresses at either end of the Great Glen, at Inverlochy and Inverness. Nothing like these bastioned forts, called citadels, had been seen before in the Highlands. They were the shape of things to come.

PEACE UNDER FIRE

On Charles II's return to his thrones in 1660, the garrisons were removed and the forts slighted. But the fragile peace was exposed after the deposition of Charles's brother, James VII and II. James's replacements, William and Mary, were seen by many in Scotland as foreign usurpers. Their avowed Protestantism added to the disaffection amongst the predominantly Catholic and Episcopalian Highland clans. William and Mary had no choice but to return to Cromwell's tactics of military occupation. Inverlochy Citadel was rebuilt and renamed Fort William, and Inverness Castle was strengthened.

The clamour to return the Stuarts to the throne only increased among the Jacobites when the Hanoverian George I became king in 1714. Jacobite uprisings in 1715 and 1719 led the British government to undertake a flurry of building. Initially, four infantry barracks were built to support Fort William and Inverness Castle. Then, following Major-General Wade's arrival in Scotland in 1724, a network of military roads was put in place, as well as a new fort – Fort Augustus – at the south end of Loch Ness and major new buildings and defences at Inverness Castle, now renamed Fort George.

Above right: Ruthven Barracks, near Kingussie, was one of four infantry barracks built after the Jacobite Risings of 1715 and 1719. It fell to the Jacobites in 1746, shortly before the battle of Culloden.

TIMELINE

1650	1725

OLIVER CROMWELL invades Scotland and builds fortresses at Inverlochy (now Fort William) and Inverness.

MAJOR-GENERAL GEORGE WADE recommends building new forts at Fort Augustus and Inverness (the first Fort George).

FROM CULLODEN TO FORT GEORGE

The Jacobites were not impressed by the Hanoverians' military building programme. Early in the 1745–6 Rising, Prince Charles Edward Stuart's army ignored the Great Glen forts as they headed south. On their return from Derby, and by now equipped with heavy guns stolen from the Hanoverian army, they laid siege to them. Fort George (Inverness) fell easily. A lucky shell detonated Fort Augustus's powder magazine and its commander immediately surrendered. Only Fort William held out.

Below: An engraving of the battle of Culloden, first published only two years after the battle itself. The picture is clearly anti-Jacobite: the British redcoats (so-called for the bright attire) stand in order while the Jacobites charge chaotically across the centre of the field.

But Bonnie Prince Charlie's humiliating defeat at Culloden, on 16 April 1746, ended all Jacobite hopes of further resistance. For the victorious Hanoverians, meanwhile, the smoking ruins of Fort Augustus and Fort George provided a cautionary spectacle. All their previous measures had proved ineffective. The martial prowess of the Highlanders would not be underestimated next time by George II's government.

Ambitious plans were drawn up to greatly extend the network of military roads. Medieval castles across the Highlands and Islands were converted into barracks, from which 'redcoats' could patrol the straths and glens, and Fort Augustus was repaired. The situation in Inverness proved more complicated. It was clear that Fort George would have to be abandoned – the question was where to put its replacement. A scheme for reconstructing Cromwell's citadel down by the harbour was aborted when the burgh council claimed compensation for its loss. The thought of having 2,000 'wild and licentious' soldiers foisted on the ladies of Inverness also proved too much. In desperation, the Duke of Cumberland instructed Lieutenant-General Skinner, newly appointed military engineer for Scotland, to look elsewhere. Skinner alighted on a barren spit of land jutting into the Moray Firth at Ardersier, 11 miles east of Inverness. This would be the site of the second Fort George.

Above: The military road over the Grampian Mountains, looking towards Corgarff. The Hanoverian government planned its extensive network of military roads to open up the Highlands, making control of the region easier.

1746

FORT GEORGE
(INVERNESS)
is easily captured by the Jacobites in the days leading up to the battle of Culloden.

1747

FORT GEORGE
(ARDERSIER)
is planned to serve as George II's chief garrison fortress in the Highlands.

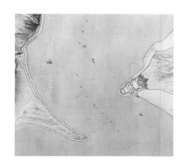

THE ARCHITECTURE OF WARFARE

Lieutenant-General William Skinner, the engineer who designed Fort George, was born in the West Indies in 1700. Orphaned early in life, he was brought up by an aunt who was married to the military engineer Talbot Edwards. Skinner trained as an engineer at the Tower of London before serving in Minorca and Gibraltar. He was at the top of his profession when in 1747 he was appointed military engineer for north Britain. Chief amongst his numerous projects was Fort George, and in recognition of his services he was appointed the fort's first governor.

In planning the defences at Fort George, Skinner adopted design principles formulated in Italy in the 16th century and subsequently honed by generations of military engineers across Europe. High masonry walls with projecting towers had been the defensive norm throughout the middle ages. They were developed to resist siege by large armies equipped with artillery that catapulted large projectiles at or over the defences. But all this was set to change when gunpowdered artillery was introduced into Europe in the 14th century.

Above: Looking eastwards from the sentry box on Prince Edward's Ravelin. The design of Fort George drew on continental models but demonstrated much innovation.

The first guns were of limited effectiveness, but as the technology improved so the builders of fortifications had to produce new defensive solutions. Because gunpowdered artillery mostly fired low and direct, they came up with an angle-bastioned defence called *Trace Italienne*. Angle-bastioned defences involved banked-up earthen ramparts, which dissipated energy from a cannonball much more effectively than masonry walls. The angled bastions themselves projected from the rampart and were of the same height – and so were far less vulnerable and more effective than tall towers.

For Fort George, Skinner used this international vocabulary of the architecture of warfare superbly, choosing those elements that lent themselves best to defending a promontory. Concentrating on the fort's landward approach, he mapped out a complex and fascinating interplay of ramparts and massive bastions, ditches and firing steps, leaving the remaining seaward sides protected by long stretches of rampart and smaller bastions.

Below: Skinner's 1747 design for Fort George. The pink rectangle on the far left of the plan denotes the only standing structure on 'this barren, sandy point' at this time – a fisherman's hut on the earl of Cawdor's estate.

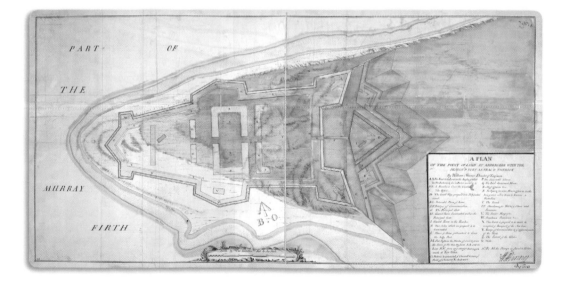

1747

SKINNER'S APPOINTMENT
William Skinner is appointed military engineer for north Britain.

1748

FROM PLANNING TO BUILDING
Skinner draws up detailed plans for Fort George (Ardersier), and building commences.

BUILDING THE FORT

The building contract for the fort was won by the famous architect William Adam, who had previously carried out work at Edinburgh Castle and the other royal castles. Yet by the time the first sod was cut at the fort, in June 1748, William was dead and his eldest son John took over. For the next 20 years, Fort George dominated the family business and involved John's other brothers, including Robert, who subsequently became one of Britain's most famous architects.

Building Fort George was a logistical nightmare. The fort covered 42 acres (17ha), the main rampart was over 1km long and the garrison buildings inside approximated to a small town. Even in normal conditions the task would have been Herculean, but the circumstances in 1748 were far from normal. Construction got underway during an uneasy and enforced peace, and the site chosen was remote from infrastructure such as roads and harbours. Although there was plenty of local labour as well as soldiers, skilled tradesmen had to be brought up from the Lowlands. Almost all the building materials had to be brought in by sea – only the thousands of bricks were made on site.

COSTLY ENTERPRISE

Practicalities were handled first. The workers and soldiers camped out on the heath behind a secure palisade, brick kilns were built and a pier and harbour constructed for deliveries. Records kept by the paymaster give an insight into the scale of works during the fort's construction, as well as the problems faced daily and the rate of progress over the years. We learn that the workforce of 'soldiers and countrymen' piling up earth for the rampart and bastion initially comprised 1,000 men, but by 1757 had dwindled to 200. The final cost of building the fort was more than £200,000, about £20 million at today's prices and more than Scotland's annual Gross National Product for 1750.

Above: Lieutenant-Colonel James Wolfe visited Fort George in 1751 during its construction. He was complimentary about the works, but less so about the soldiers building it. 'They frequently kill their officers through fear,' Wolfe wrote, 'and murder one another in confusion.'

FROM START TO FINISH

1748 Outworks, ravelin and ditches begun.

1749 Glacis completed.

1751 Main rampart and eastern bastions begun.

1753 Ravelin and ravelin guardhouse completed. Principal gate begun. Barrack foundations laid.

1754 Ravelin armed with eight 12-pounders, with a further eight placed on the great mounds of earth forming the eastern bastions.

1756 Principal gate finished.

1757 Central pavilion of north barracks ready. Grand magazine foundations laid.

1758 Rampart complete up to height of stone cordon. Prince of Wales's and Duke of Cumberland's bastions complete to parapets. Last sods of turf laid on covered way.

1759 Grand magazine completed. Ordnance stores foundations laid.

1760 Points magazine and casemates completed. Provision stores foundations completed.

1761 Ordnance stores and north barracks completed. Staff block foundations laid. Places of arms outside sallyports begun.

1762 Casemates and provision stores completed. Artillery block and workshops begun. Fort receives its main armament.

1763 Garrison chapel foundations laid.

1765 Places of arms outside sallyports completed. Principal bridge begun.

1766 Staff and artillery blocks completed. Principal bridge completed and principal gates hung. Heath beyond glacis cleared and flattened to improve line of fire.

1767 Garrison chapel and south barracks completed.

1768 Minor works and fitting out of interiors.

1769 Fort George effectively completed.

DAILY ROUTINE

Soldiers at Fort George lived according to strict routine, as this daily timetable for an 18th-century private shows. Disobedience was heavily disciplined. In 1831 David Abernethy was sentenced to 60 days for being drunk on guard. He recorded his name, crime and punishment (far right) while in the prison behind the officers' guardroom.

05.00	Get out of bed, do chores
06.00	Drill
07.45	Breakfast in barrack room
10.00	More drill
12.00	Dinner in barrack room
14.00	More drill
16.00	Tea and back to the barrack room

A SOLDIER'S LIFE

In the late 18th century an ever-extending British empire created a constant need for army recruits. Taking 'the king's shilling' took many a young Highlander out of poverty and back into Highland dress (proscribed for civilians after Culloden). But it was a hard, tedious and very poorly paid life. A soldier received a shilling per week in wages. From this he had to find money for food, equipment and clothing. This left many a soldier with next-to-nothing to keep a family, or to send back home – far less to save for the future.

DOMESTIC CONFLICT

Barrack life was heavily regulated. Few men were permitted to marry, and for those who were, their wives faced years without a home, able to earn only half rations by doing regimental chores. Before married quarters became the norm from the mid-19th century, if there were no spare rooms in barracks the couple would be given a bed in the corner of a barrack room with a blanket as their only privacy. Children slept where they could, and in the garrison orders for Fort George there is a constant battle to keep children in order – regulations to stop them breaking windows, making a noise, interfering with the guns, using the ramparts as a toilet, playing ball games in the barracks and remaining in barracks when sick.

Drink and boredom were the greatest evils. Standing orders for the sentries at Fort George in 1808 charged them to prevent 'whisky women' from entering the fort. Even at the hospital door the guards were expressly ordered to prevent liquor from being carried in.

Above: This detail from an 18th-century painting by David Morier depicts a soldier of the 42nd Highland Regiment in full Highland dress.

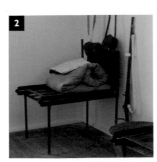

Opposite: Metal turn-up beds, dating from the 1880s, in the main guardroom; **(1)** kettle, hob and stove in the 1780 barrack room; **(2)** replica fold-up bed and mattress; and **(3)** oil lamp, both in the 1868 barrack room.

A TRAINING BASE

The regiments despatched to Fort George immediately after 1769 served as its garrison and provided patrols out-stationed throughout the straths and glens. But once the Hanoverian government perceived that the Jacobite threat was over it established a new use for the fort – as a training base. Most of the newly-raised Highland regiments spent a few weeks there, doing basic training and getting equipped before leaving for all corners of the empire.

In 1766 Prime Minister William Pitt, in a letter to George III, wrote this about the Highland recruits: 'It is my boast that I was the first minister who looked for merit and found it in the mountains of the north. I called it forth, and drew into your service a hardy and intrepid race of men, who became a prey to the artifice of your enemies, and had gone nigh to have

Above: Soldiers of the Highland Rifle Militia, photographed at Fort George in about 1869.

overturned the State. These men … were brought to combat on your side; they served with fidelity, as they fought with valour, and conquered for you in every part of the world.'

The pressing need for recruits meant that by 1795 the garrisoning role at the fort was given to the 'Invalids Company' – men unfit for active service but capable of garrison duty. This 18th-century 'Dad's Army' was supported by a company of artillery, who kept the fort's guns in readiness for action that never came.

FORT MISERY

Few visitors came to the fort, thanks to its remoteness. Perhaps the best known were Dr Samuel Johnston and James Boswell in August 1773, as guests of the governor. Johnston later wrote: 'I could not help being struck with some admiration, in finding upon this barren sandy point, such buildings – such a dinner – such company; it was like enchantment.'

'Enchantment' was not exactly the word most soldiers sent to Fort George used to describe it. The fort was so remote that soldiers came to know it as 'Fort Misery'. Private James Anton, in 1812, perhaps summed up the collective opinion of most when he wrote in a letter home: 'Fort George is so remotely situated that few soldiers like to be quartered within its walls.'

So remote was the fort to the London-based government's way of thinking that they even considered it suitable as a prison for Napoleon following his capture at Waterloo! The fort had not long before served as a detention place for Irish political prisoners captured in the Wexford Rising of 1798.

Above: A soldier of the Invalids Regiment, which manned the fort in the late 18th century.

1773

JOHNSON AND BOSWELL visit the fort and dine with the governor, Sir Eyre Coote.

1798

IRISH POLITICAL PRISONERS from the Wexford Rising are imprisoned in Fort George.

A COASTAL DEFENCE BATTERY

By 1800, Fort George's effectiveness as a fortification was in question. Improved artillery, especially the invention of the shrapnel shell, meant that the landward side was now uncomfortably dominated by the high ground beyond it. The place could no longer be considered 'state of the art'.

After Waterloo in 1815, the fort was even in danger of being 'pensioned off' when an order to dismantle all the Highland forts was given, then countermanded. In 1835 a government proposal to convert the fort into a prison came to nothing.

It was the outbreak of the Crimea War with Russia in 1854 that shook a complacent nation to its roots, saw the revival of home militia regiments and came to the rescue of Fort George. The Ross-shire and Inverness-shire militias both regularly exercised there in the 1850s. Then in 1859 came Emperor Napoleon III's invasion threat, putting pressure on the towns and forts along the British coast to look to their defences. As a result, Fort George, guarding the narrow channel to Inverness, was refortified with a powerful coastal-defence battery. The entire seaward side was radically rearmed with the latest military hardware.

REGIMENTAL DEPOT

The 1881 'root and branch' reorganisation of the army infused new life into Fort George. It became the depot of the Seaforth Highlanders, no strangers to Fort George. The Seaforths were an amalgamation of the 72nd and 78th Highlanders, and the 78th had first paraded at the fort in July 1793 shortly after its formation.

Fort George continued as the regimental depot until 1961 when the regiment was amalgamated with the Cameron Highlanders to form the Queen's Own Highlanders. (They have since amalgamated with the Gordon Highlanders to become the Highlanders, the Royal Regiment of Scotland.) When the Queen's Own Highlanders marched out of the fort in 1964, following another major army reorganisation, the connection was not severed, for their Regimental Association and Museum remained in the fort. They are there to this day.

Above: The memorial at Fort George to the 8,432 soldiers and officers of the Seaforth Highlanders who lost their lives in the First World War.

Opposite: The sentry box atop Prince Henry Frederick's bastion, looking towards the Duke of Marlborough's demi-bastion. Fears of a French coastal invasion in 1859 meant that the entire seaward side of the fort was heavily rearmed, with two 68-pounder cannon and seven 10-inch guns.

1860

1881

FRENCH THREAT
Fears of invasion result in Fort George being rearmed as a coastal defence battery.

SEAFORTH HIGHLANDERS
The Seaforths take over Fort George as their regimental depot.

Fort George is one of over 40 Historic Scotland sites in north-east Scotland, a selection of which is shown below.

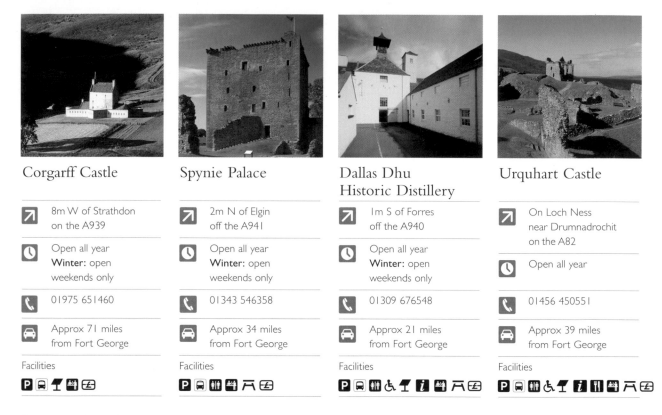

Corgarff Castle

↗	8m W of Strathdon on the A939
🕐	Open all year **Winter:** open weekends only
📞	01975 651460
🚗	Approx 71 miles from Fort George

Facilities

🅿 🚌 🍴 ⛺ ♿

Spynie Palace

↗	2m N of Elgin off the A941
🕐	Open all year **Winter:** open weekends only
📞	01343 546358
🚗	Approx 34 miles from Fort George

Facilities

🅿 🚌 🚻 ⛺ 🏔 ♿

Dallas Dhu Historic Distillery

↗	1m S of Forres off the A940
🕐	Open all year **Winter:** open weekends only
📞	01309 676548
🚗	Approx 21 miles from Fort George

Facilities

🅿 🚌 🚻 ♿ 🍴 ℹ ⛺ 🏔 ♿

Urquhart Castle

↗	On Loch Ness near Drumnadrochit on the A82
🕐	Open all year
📞	01456 450551
🚗	Approx 39 miles from Fort George

Facilities

🅿 🚌 🚻 ♿ 🍴 ℹ 🍽 ⛺ 🏔 ♿

For more information on all Historic Scotland sites, visit **www.historic-scotland.gov.uk**
To order tickets and a wide range of gifts, visit **www.historic-scotland.gov.uk/shop**

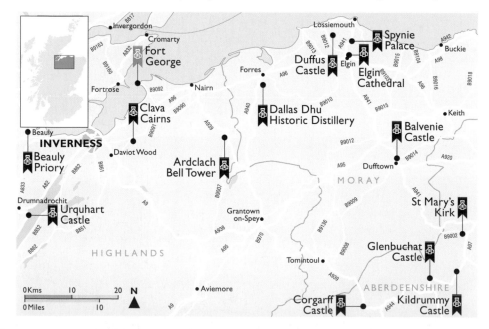

Key to facilities

Admission charge	💷
Bus/coach parking	🚌
Car parking	🅿
Interpretive display	🍴
Picnic area	🏔
Reasonable wheelchair access	♿
Shop	🛍
Cafe/restaurant	🍽
Toilets	🚻
Visitor centre	ℹ

Strong footwear is recommended at Corgarff Castle.